Dreadful Wind & Rain

Dreadful Wind & Rain

a lyric narrative

Diane Gilliam

Red Hen Press | *Pasadena, CA*

Dreadful Wind & Rain
Copyright © 2017 by Diane Gilliam
All Rights Reserved

No part of this book may be used or reproduced in any manner whatsoever without the prior written permission of both the publisher and the copyright owner.

Book layout by Cierra Coppini

Library of Congress Cataloging-in-Publication Data

Names: Gilliam, Diane, author.
Title: Dreadful wind & rain : a lyric narrative / Diane Gilliam.
Description: First edition. | Pasadena, CA : Red Hen Press, 2017. |
  Includes bibliographical references.
Identifiers: LCCN 2016048363 | ISBN 9781597097499 (pbk. : alk. paper)
Classification: LCC PS3607.I44445 D74 2017 | DDC 811/.6—dc23
LC record available at https://lccn.loc.gov/2016048363

The National Endowment for the Arts, the Los Angeles County Arts Commission, the Dwight Stuart Youth Foundation, the Max Factor Family Foundation, the Pasadena Tournament of Roses Foundation, the Pasadena Arts & Culture Commission and the City of Pasadena Cultural Affairs Division, the City of Los Angeles Department of Cultural Affairs, the Audrey & Sydney Irmas Charitable Foundation, Sony Pictures Entertainment, Amazon Literary Partnership, and the Sherwood Foundation partially support Red Hen Press.

First Edition
Published by Red Hen Press
www.redhen.org

*For Darlene, Eleanor, George Ella, and Kumkum,
who stayed right with me*

Contents

I. *Girl*

    13 ... Girl
    14 ... Tale
    16 ... The Father's Story
    17 ... Favorite Dress
    18 ... The Bargain
    19 ... Something About Leah
    22 ... The Naming of the Scars
    24 ... Shadow Play
    26 ... The Knot
    28 ... Once

II. *Anyone*

    31 ... Tender
    33 ... His and Hers
    34 ... The Fairest of Them All
    35 ... The Message
    36 ... Threshold
    37 ... *Leah Will Say Nothing*
    39 ... Horror
    40 ... Driving Home From the Store, He Says *Your Sister Called*
    41 ... Except Through Me
    42 ... Ringstraked
    43 ... The Heart
    44 ... All That Drowned Beauty
    45 ... Bluebeard Variation
    46 ... The Twelfth Wise Woman
    47 ... Now
    48 ... For Goodness Sake
    50 ... *Oh, Honey*
    52 ... Fair and Tender Ladies
    54 ... First Divorce

III. *Or Else*

    57 ... Deed
    59 ... On the Silence of Cotton
    60 ... She Starts To Slow Down
    61 ... Still Joy
    63 ... Harvest
    66 ... Three Things That Happened Yesterday
    68 ... Lots of Ships
    69 ... It's Not Up To You, Sweetheart
    70 ... Small Song, or, Cosmology
    71 ... How I Don't Know
    72 ... Some Things the Doorways Want To Tell Us
    73 ... Maybe This Will Help
    75 ... Where I'm From
    77 ... An Invisible Story
    78 ... Or Else
    79 ... The Apple
    80 ... Sorting the Seeds
    82 ... Way Down at the Bottom of Everything
           Where It's All Mixed Up and Everyone
              Is Everyone
    83 ... Begotten
    85 ... Stones

IV. *After*

    89 ... Psalm of Leah
    90 ... I and Thou
    91 ... Soul Retrieval
    92 ... Leaving the Story

    93 ... Notes

There were two sisters of County Clare
Oh the wind and the rain
One was dark and the other was fair
Oh the dreadful wind and rain

—Traditional

I

Girl

Girl

Whatever it is she is wanting, it is not
too much to ask. We would give it to her
if we could, now we are grown women in a car
outside the small yellow house where she is forever
fifteen, forever leaning her elbows on the front
windowsill, pretending not to watch
for whatever it is she's wanting.

The living room curtains are closed
behind her. Behind her, her mother and sister
are fighting. *Your sister waged a war in that house*, is how the mother
will tell the story years later. *Your dad was her ally, and I
was her enemy. And you were nothing*, the mother
will say. *And I was nothing*,
the girl will say.

She knows better than to ask
for whatever it is she's wanting. We would give her
another story if we could, now we are grown women in a car
on our way to somewhere else. She was nothing, so her story, I'm trying
to explain, comes disguised as no story at all. And if I still can't say
what it is I am wanting, look closely at the windowpane,
it's what I brought you here to see—how it holds us
in that house apart from what we want,
how the glass makes it look
like there is nothing
to stop us
at all.

Tale

Someone put my mother in a box.

This is an old story.

The box could have been gold
or glass or ice. It was a cedar chest
weighted with blankets and quilts
for a family of ten. He took them out
and put her in, she was three maybe four.
He told her not to move, pressed the quilts
and blankets down on her face
and the box clicked shut.

This was after. This is the story
of the sins of the brother, hand-me-down
version of the sins of the father.

They searched first the yard inside
the fence, then the wood. They went
up the mountain, into the old bear cave
back of the house. They called, they shouted.
They tore their hair.

He'd told her not to move.

Every tale has its local inflections.
Hers could have ended with kindly strangers,
a woodsman and his wife longing
for a child of their own. Instead, it was
a whipping for the hiding and the scare.

This is a long story.

The brother long since dead,
the box, of course, still alive, dark heirloom
crouched in the corners of all our rooms.

We walk by, something clicks
and whispers,
        Don't move.

The Father's Story

Back then, people knew how to make
something out of nothing. If there wasn't grass,
women'd go out with a broom and sweep
a pattern, like fan quilting, in their dirt.
If there was a stump in the yard,
there'd be an ax stuck in it, with a handle
somebody's grandfather'd carved
all winter by the fire with a piece of broken glass.
My mom was cutting lace
out of newspapers to line the cupboard shelves
when she told me they were sending me
to live with Aunt Vi and Uncle Jim.
They didn't have any kids to work their farm
and they were, hands down,
the meanest people that ever lived.
I'd be out hoeing corn and hear the school bell.
I loved to read, everything I could get my hands on,
but they wouldn't let me go, even in winter.
Once I found some old rusty wheels in the barn.
I thought to build a wheelbarrow
to carry the stove wood up to the porch
from the field. Uncle Jim pitched a fit,
called me a thieving son-of-a-bitch
on account of those wheels. Man, oh, man.
They knew how to take something, too,
and turn it into nothing.

Favorite Dress

I had a dress that was yellow. This was when I was six, and the dress was size six. The top part was plain, yellow, the neck was round, and it had no sleeves. It was a light yellow—like butter, not margarine, just this side of white. The skirt was gathered, it gathered swirls of pink and blue into the yellow. At school we learned about the color wheel, how white was all colors. I knew if I twirled fast enough, I could turn the pink and blue and yellow in my dress into white and I would be like a cloud—I would be all the colors at once.

The Bargain

> *In all the variations of the story [of the Handless Maiden]*
> *the daughter does not object.*
> —Robert Johnson

I want to talk to you about something grown-up, the Father says. Your sister hasn't been feeling very happy, you know she doesn't get the same kinds of grades as you, or have the same kinds of friends. You're so special that sometimes she feels like she's not. I want her to feel like we're on her side so what we're going to do is, we're not going to brag on you so much and we're going to talk her up a whole lot more. I know I can tell you this even though you're only seven, so when it happens you'll understand. We love you the same and we don't want you to change, but we're going to have to chop off your hands.

Something About Leah

> *And Laban had two daughters: the name of the elder was Leah, and the name of the younger was Rachel.*
>
> *Leah was tender-eyed, but Rachel was beautiful and well-favoured.*
> —Genesis 28:16-17

Rachel is beautiful,
my mother's oldest sister says
to Mother, *but there is something
about Leah.*

I catch my breath
to hear what it is, but Mother
doesn't answer and aunt Tikva
says no more.

They are at their weaving—
every year the big visit
of the seven sisters. They come
to sit in their circle and tell secrets,
weave new headscarves
for all the daughters. They know
everything I don't.

There is no fire at the center
of their circle, but it is warm there
as a lap full of babies. They don't
eat sweets while they weave,
but when I hide around their edges
I think they laugh like honey cakes
are filling their mouths—aunt Tikva,
sometimes she laughs so hard
she tips sideways
into my mother's shoulder

and not even Mother can sit
up straight against that. Their hands
are beautiful in the threads, quick
as birds with many wings and when
I'm alone, I try to make my hands
fly like theirs. I am twelve, it is almost
my time. My breasts will grow
and my blood will come
and Mother will have to
let me in. Now, when she sees me,
she says, *Leah, go find your sister.*
I beg, *I beg* her to let me stay.
I fly my fingers like little birds
to show I can be useful, I can
be trusted with the thread,
I could make my own.

Even when aunt Tikva says,
Oh, Adah, let her stay, Mother
looks at me hard and says, *You go
find your sister, Leah. Rachel
will be lonely.* So I have to go.
But Rachel makes fun of aunt Tikva
and the other sisters, and me.
Let her be lonely, is what I say.

They have finished Rachel's scarf.
She likes squares and triangles
made into patterns like stars.
I like waves, and bird wings, and circles
more than squares. I like the moon
better than the stars. *Now, then,*
aunt Tikva says as she runs

her hand over Rachel's scarf
still lying across Mother's lap,
what shall we do for Leah?

The Naming of the Scars

1.

Just above the right eyebrow
   where I missed, getting into
      the family car.

White crescent moons on my forearms
   where my sister's fingernails pressed in hard.

The silvery blur at the crinkled edge
   of the backyard black and white
      is me trying to get myself
         out of the picture.

It's a problem, where to go to cry
   in a very small house. My sister's eyes
      and ears quickened after me.
         I can swallow anything now
            without making a sound.

2.

The glossy dent around the finger
   from the twenty-five year ring.

Glassy skin of the bathroom mirror
   where you could not feel your face
      before you went downstairs and let him
         get away with everything.

The made bed, the unmade kitchen
   the lamp slammed to the floor
      the stain on the rug, the stain on the sheet
         the broken wall.

The skin gone soft and pocked
   around the mouth is how worry taps
      and taps at the face and keeps the mouth
         from what it would say.

There is a posture of shrinkage
   in which it all draws in
      and the husband and the sister
         win.

3.

In the waiting room before they can tell you
what has gone wrong, they give you
a drawing of a body, like an outline
drawn in chalk on the floor, only this one
they've made is straight and strong.
Mark in blue, the instructions say,
the places that are numb.

Shadow Play

1.

Early morning when the shadows
are so long it feels like everything
is all pulled out of itself,
Rachel and I walk to the fields,
our long selves laid out ahead of us
for anyone to see.

Rachel likes to get behind me
so our two shadows look like one,
then she waves her arms, or makes horns
on my shadow head and grunts,
or puts her head on my shoulder
and makes me into some kind
of two-headed monster. Every time,
it makes me twist my face
in like a fist, then Rachel hops
around in front, walking and
skipping backwards the rest
of the way, watching my face,
—*my face I try to keep for my own*—
her dark eyes pecking at me
like a sharp little bird.

2.

Every noontime
when the sun
is exactly
over my head,
I stop
what I'm doing.
I stand
perfectly
straight.
I don't
breathe.
I look
without
moving
a muscle
in my body
at the brightness
all around
my feet.
I don't care
if my skin
blisters.

At such
moments,
almost,
I have no
sister.

The Knot

1.

The girl is given a knot
of thread the size of a boulder
with no beginning and no end and told
to wind it into a proper skein suited
for weaving by morning. The prize,
of course, is marriage.

2.

She is only ten, fifth grade,
it is the year somebody's mom
comes to her class once a week to teach
the girls to knit. She wants to make something.
It's the year of no money so she chooses it
for herself—not the smooth-skeined
Red Heart that unspools cleanly from its center,
but Aunt Lydia's Rug Yarn,
only thirty-nine cents a skein, meant to be cut
into finger-length pieces and knotted
into stiff canvas mesh, then put on the floor
and walked on. She wants to make
anything.
        You take what you get.
A loose-looped mess she'd have to untangle
and roll into a ball before she could take it
to school. All weekend on the living room floor
with yard-long tangles and knots the size
of softballs. One loop drawn free
brings on a paroxysm of snarl

somewhere else down the line.
All weekend on the floor.
She could fix it, she would fix it.
Don't try to stop her.

3.

Decades later, on her way out the door,
she still is looking for the why of it all,
believing now that the husband was really
trying to get rid of her from the start.

She insists on an answer.

All he can say is this—
he doesn't know why,
but he thinks he loves her
when he sees her working for hours
on something all laid out on the floor,
down on her hands and knees,
with next to nothing
of something impossible,
trying to make it work
and willing for anything.

Once

did my mother see me, early evening in summer
just before lamplighting time. Fourteen or fifteen,
I sat leaning against the doorway, facing the darker,
bluer side of the sky, where the crooked road from the east
reaches over the mountainside. I was almost hidden,
that must have been why she slowed and stopped
or maybe she had only turned from her hurry
to look for a moment at the last of the sun.
She smiled a little, the air was cool
and still as the water in the well
beneath the unlifted stone.

Are you looking for something, Leah?
she said, and I gave her my full, real eyes
though already she was looking
back toward the sun.
Yes, I told her.
Anyone.

II

Anyone

Tender

Loving him is too much
cereal and milk
when what she wants

are platters of fried eggs and ham,
biscuits and gravy, fried apples
in big steaming bowls,

sudden storms of sliced
potatoes and slivered onions
hitting hot grease

in heavy black skillets—
and someone
pushing it all at her, saying

Eat, eat.
He's a tune that devils her,
whose words

she can't quite capture—
something
about two sisters,

dreadful wind
and rain; he's a poem
she wrote in a dream

that faded like bruises
from the page. His eyes murky
as windows of a second-hand store

in a strange town, with what looks
like the exact quilt, one of a kind
pitcher, out of print record

she has been wanting
for years—
just closing as she pulls

into the lot, shades drawn
before she's run halfway,
even though she is willing

and has money to pay.

His and Hers

She cannot imagine it otherwise.
She wakes in the morning and twists her ring,
loves how every night in their bed he lies

breathing warm in the dark and never shies
away. He lets her talk, he lets her sing.
She cannot imagine it otherwise.

One night she's surprised how gently he tries
to move her arm when he thinks she's sleeping.
In the night, in their bed, she sees he lies

watching the ceiling long before sunrise.
Too much coffee, too many late nights working.
She cannot imagine it otherwise.

He quiets. The more she worries and pries
the less he tells her about anything.
She's sure every night in their bed he lies

wanting a room beyond reach of her eyes.
He sighs—she cries so much, *Over nothing*.
She cannot imagine it otherwise:
Every night in their bed, he lies.

The Fairest of Them All

I'm a little worried about him, says the mother-in-law when she calls. He's not making the kind of progress he should, he's still in chapter two last I heard. If he's gotten two extensions from the graduate school, will they give him a third? So what I'm thinking is, since you're almost done, you could slow down, even stop for awhile, maybe till fall. Even if it doesn't help him go faster, he could still catch up and feel like he's doing well. I am only trying to think what would be fairest to us all.

The Message

One morning the husband got up so cheerful and said to the wife, "I'll drive the girls to your sister's today so you can get to school early and do your work." Now, this struck the wife as odd for two reasons—first because the husband was never cheerful and second because it was not like him to offer to do anything that seemed like work, such as driving the little girls to her sister's who was a babysitter for a living. She wanted to accept his offer but something inside her was dragging its feet. So, quickly she thought, and said, "No, I have a special order in at the bookstore. I'll take the girls and pick it up on the way." "Oh," said the husband and walked away looking decidedly less cheerful.

The wife gathered up her books and keys and girls and was about to walk out the door when the husband reappeared. He had in his hand a stack of paper and a bag of coffee. "I promised to take her these," he said. "She wants to write a resume and she is out of coffee." The wife looked at the husband's face then she tucked the paper and coffee under her arm and left.

By the time she drew near to her sister's, the thing that dragged its feet had begun to rattle its chains and moan. She pulled into the apartment parking lot from the side that couldn't be seen from her sister's door. The little girls ran on ahead while she gathered up the paper and coffee. When she got to the door her little girls were already inside. The sister was sitting on the couch dressed in such a way and sitting in such a way, expecting the husband to come through the door. "He sent you these," the wife said when she was inside, handing the sister the coffee and paper, over the din of the thing inside that wailed and thrashed and groaned. "Oh, how sweet," said the sister as she turned and smiled in such a way that was the Devil's own.

Threshold

She sits on the ground,
two, maybe three, waiting
for daddy to carry her

across a lake of black mud
flooding the yard.
Or else it's now

and she's sitting on her own
front curb. Her husband
has gone inside. She can't

remember exactly
what he said.
Virus.

*How does the doctor
think you got it?*
she'd asked him.

She looks up
from her hands,
crossed over her chest,

back at her house,
then toward the street.
Rocks herself

while she can
between
the before

and the after.

Leah Will Say Nothing

my father said, *when Jacob enters
the tent, until it is accomplished.*
I did not believe it would be
accomplished. What thief
does not know trickery when it comes
courting, hands full of daughters,
and sheep, and savoury meat?
Yet he came into the tent in the dark,
full of intention and heat. My body
would not have it, my gorge rose against him, and I said,

Jacob.

Straightway he began to rage and wring,
flail and hit, twist my hair around his fist
to hold me. He hurt me, however he could
he hurt me, like gutting one of my father's sheep
with no thought of the life,
only the meat.

        Then in the morning,
great weeping and wailing and beating
of breasts, the show for Rachel.
Jacob and my father dealing, Mother
comforting Rachel.

        My body wept
and wept, it could not stop knowing.
No eyes followed me from the tent
to the well. The knife was sharp
and hard but finally, I could not.
With my eyes, I stared

at the four of them, eating now
outside the tent, and with my mouth
I cursed them
    as I keened
        and the knife
            sawed off my hair.

Horror

Her hand is on fire
as it moves,
mechanical,
slowly toward
the doorknob.

The rest of her
is somewhere else.

He's on the other side
of the door. There was begging
on the phone, there was crying.
There are two little girls
in clean summer pajamas
upstairs in their beds.
The door is locked.
He's crying, he's knocking.

She's about
to do it, like all the girls
in the movies who see
something in the dark
in a mask, hear something
with a buzz saw
and a hunger for life out
in the bushes and
    —her hand,
        her hand is screaming—
they open the door and
they feed it.

Driving Home From the Store, He Says *Your Sister Called*

It was her, he says. *You know
I never could tell you apart
on the phone. I talked to her
for fifteen minutes, all the time thinking
it was you. Neither of us realized
until I asked when you'd be home.
She didn't see it coming,* he says.
She took it hard.
                      Quick brown flutter
and crack—an ordinary bird
flies headlong into the windshield, topples
over the roof of the car. He pulls over, gets out
and walks back down the road to look
for the body. *Don't you hate
when that happens?* he says,
hunched over the steering wheel, crying.
No, she tells him, looking the other way.
I don't care it's dead.

Except Through Me

Jacob's hunger for this first son
urges him to my side at every pause
in the day, the way Esau's hunger
after days and nights on the mountain
must have urged him on to Jacob's fire,
the simmering pot casting a wide
fragrant net, luring the brother
with the empty belly.
                              But my belly
is not empty. Jacob kneels and lays
his palms on either side of the heavy
undercurve of the baby's bowl as if
to drink, as if it were a whole world
that he holds. He whispers, he presses
his ear against my side as if to hear. I know
it is not meant for me—the promise, the light
on the face, the love in the hands.
Still, for hours my skin glows
where I have been touched by the love
and the light, and in this story I do not
know which one I am—the thief by the fire
or the starved one clutching the birthright.

Ringstraked

The morning Jacob called us to the field
and said he would take us back
to the land of his father, Isaac—
the one led up the mountain by his father
to be bound and knifed and burnt for love
of the god of his fathers, I thought,
I will not.

I would stay, I would put away the knife
I'd kept after that first night.
Small at first, twisted flick of the tip
around the white crescent scars
Rachel's fingernails left on my forearms
when we were girls. Then deeper
lines inside my thighs, the parts
he used against me.

We would go, he said, then he knelt
and started on the green poplar rods. He scored
and ringed and nicked them till the white
shone through, freckled and blotched,
then he laid them in the gutters of the troughs
—he believes with this he makes the cattle
bear young of the same mottled stripe.
This wage I have settled with your father, Leah,
he said to me aside. *Those born solid
stay with him. The speckled and spotted
and ringstraked are mine.*

The Heart

When they cut it out, they were surprised
to see what a tangled mess it was,
a jerry-rigged thing, like someone had pulled
all the wires out of the distributor cap and someone else
who barely knew what to do had tried to put it
all back, twisting on new bits
of wire to keep the connections alive,
to keep the heart beating
in that gnarl of barbed wire.

And she was surprised
to find out it was true, the story
she'd been telling for years, the one
where she'd disappeared into the wood,
where someone wanted to get something for nothing
and she was the nothing
because always there is a price to be paid

and only her heart would do.

All That Drowned Beauty

The moon, maybe, was trying to tell us
what happens to girls who go down
by the river at night, trying to throw light
on each small disturbance of the water
as though each wavelet were a girl
coming up for the third
and last time: pretty Polly, little Omie,
the girls we were at thirteen
and seventeen and twenty-three
    —*Only say that you'll be mine . . .*

The Kanawha crawling
with coal barges, each with a carbide
trained on the black surface
of the water, mechanical
monsters patrolling a deep
we couldn't gauge.

It wanted us, that river.

We sat back from the edge
and we told. We said it all
out loud—the lying, the pushing,
the watching while we drowned.

We tossed it all out
like breadcrumbs onto the water
and watched the barges push it under again
and again. Watched, like praying, for
small circles to pock the smooth center
path of their wakes, starveling fish
                          —or girls
rising, and trying, trying
to break the black waters and live.

Bluebeard Variation

In another version of our story, it is the husband who enters the forbidden room while the wife is away, the wife having left her keys behind, as he was to take her to and from the airport for her flights. He himself tells her on the drive home that he has taken the keys and gone into her studio, though he says he didn't look at anything, or stay long, only lay on the couch as there was nothing there for him to do. His feelings, of course, are terribly hurt that she does not take the violation well. When they stop at the studio on the way home so that she can pick up some papers, something sticky and dark puddles out onto the porch from under the door. *You left. You left your keys on the counter,* he says, and pointing at the spreading stain, *See what you made me do?*

The Twelfth Wise Woman

She comes after,
she is the last one
you are going to hear from.

When the wounding goes
beyond the pale, when your hands
are bleeding and bound, and every part
that can be hurt lies drenched in hurt, your face
swollen and bloodless and still, when

you
are the kill,

she comes in
through the dark, through the back door
of no return
to who you were before.

You cannot speak
but she takes her place and she answers, *Sleep*.
Once again you cannot speak. She picks up her work
and answers again, *As long as it takes*.

Now

> *And Leah conceived, and bare a son, and she called his name Reuben: for she said, surely the Lord hath looked upon my affliction; now therefore my husband will love me.*
> —Genesis 29:32

Now I leave off
wanting the love of my husband.
Neither can I love him, but keep with him
for the sake of my sons. I will not die
of this, nor be poor in the issue of love. If I
love my sons with all I am, does not love indwell
my house? This son I carry, he looks
to no one, calls to no one, he comes
for his own sweet sake.
I name him Judah—
Now I will praise.

For Goodness Sake

We tried and tried to get it right.
We made our beds and turned out
the lights. We sat in front and
raised our hands. We made sure—
how many pages, when it was due,
what we needed to know.

We worked hard, and we paid our own way
to the movies, to school, to exhaustion. We paid
our dearest price and we paid in advance
of whatever might make us sorry later.
We paid in pennies and nickels
out of jars, in late nights and headaches,
in things swept under the rug by brooms
we wielded—each straw by itself
enough to break our backs.

We spared our dimes for a cup
of coffee, quarters for bus fare.
We handed ones out car windows
to fathers with cardboard signs, but only
if we didn't have a five or ten. Out
of our purses we pulled our lunch money,
book money, mad money, we handed it over
to whoever needed it most and
before we knew it, we couldn't afford
to get mad, ever again.

We spared other people's feelings, we looked
the other way, we looked at all the reasons
why. We looked at both sides
of the story so no one could say
we hadn't tried. We turned our other cheek

so many times our own faces became
a blur, and we could no longer see
what was right in front of us.

And none of it added up, none of it,
for all we had put in. When we got
to the bottom line, the finishing line,
there was no balance, we could not take stock,
we could not win, no matter what we did
or said or could prove. Stunned,
we put down our hands.

After a moment,
we tucked our purses out of sight.

A stillness came
and an emptiness that made us cry at first,
but like babies, soon we understood—it was ordinary
hunger, we were hungry, like everyone else.
And that, at last, was good.

Oh, Honey

they said, as she flung her story
out on the bed, ragged flower garden
of her own making, the reds and pinks
gone first, disintegrated. Raw patches
of the quilt's underlayers showing
through, open like wounds, like something
abraded. What was meant to keep her warm
frayed or fraying or all the way gone—
though they still could see on the thin
backing of muslin the tiny stitches she'd worked
to try and hold it all together. At the foot,
razored rips where his toenails had cut.
On the other end, stitches pulled loose where he'd
clutch a handful of quilt then turn hard
away. And in-between, stains she couldn't
or wouldn't explain, the wear and tear
of what happens in a bed. *Oh, honey.*

Whether to keep it, is what she was asking.

Honey,
over each little hexagon, so sweet
the calicos—cherries and bluebirds,
boys in short pants, Scottie dogs,
little Dutch girls washing, ironing,
baking, mending. *Honey* for the tiny
trail of stitches left like breadcrumbs
inside each patch, for the cedar chest
that held it while she'd waited, for all
she'd hoped. For the garden path
of green patches between blossoms
that let her step from one

piece to the next, but stopped dead
at the edge of the bed. *Oh, honey,*

let it go. They said it again
and again, voices rising and falling
over the beauty and the ruin, soft
weight of their words warming
her cold story and the chill
morning waiting outside
the quilt. Their words falling
like sun on a clothesline,
sun on blossoms, falling and filling
the bare, tattered comb
of her quilt with a golden
food made from the flowers
themselves, sweet and hurtless
and free. *Honey.*

Fair and Tender Ladies

Come all ye fair and tender ladies
Take warning how you court young men
They're like a bright star on a summer morning
They first appear and then they're gone
   —Traditional

There was no room for us
in the house. Our bodies
became our houses and it was
lonely in there. But they came
for us there too, couldn't let
bad enough alone.

When we opened our mouths, they said,
Not to interrupt, but . . . Not to change
the subject . . . , and we stopped
trying to change it. Mornings,
they'd say, *Could I borrow you*
for a minute?—and it took us
twenty-five years to ask for a cup
of sugar in return. To take back
all the pens and pencils
we'd let them walk off with.

And when we got those back, still
we tried to write small. Smaller
and smaller, trying to fit
whole sentences onto notepads
lined for grocery lists and things
to do. Then, late one summer,

we saw something. We saw each other.
We saw each other's words and our eyes
widened. In Our Mother's house

are many mansions, and they are us. We appeared.

And now, we're gone.

First Divorce

There was a bucket, there was a wall,
there was a woman and a man.

The woman carried the bucket
and the man was the wall.
There was no place else to go.

It was a long, long time
for there was much to carry
and there was much to wall.

There was a path ran straight
from the well to the hole in the wall.
There was a path ran crooked
from the well to the wood.

There was something in the wood
bigger than the bucket.

Woe to the man, woe to the wall.
Woe to the bucket at the edge
of the wood.

III

Or Else

Deed

Let it finally be Friday, let me drive
downtown before five, park in the one
space left open in front and feed the meter
the exact change it needs. Let me go into the office,
sit and nod, unfold my check on the table
and sign. Let the line not be dotted, let it
be solid. Let it be my name.
Let it be final.

Let me pull into the driveway while
it is still light. It's well past five and well
into October and they are just about
to change the time. Saturday night
on the local news they'll remind
us all to Fall Back, but I make it in
under the wire. There is still light.
There is still time.

I am up the back porch steps, under
the awning, my hand on the back door lock
the realtor left on. Let me remember rightly
the numbers he gave me. Let this not be the dream
of the high school locker with the Master Lock
whose combination you forgot or fumbled, turning
too fast, going too far, everything you'd locked up
irretrievable, lost.
Let the lock fall open, let me leave it
on the steps for the realtor to pick up.
Let him pull up the flimsy stakes
of the sign in the yard that says I can be bought,
let him drive away. Let no Master
enter through my door.

Let the house be a disaster, I don't care.
Let the smoke-framed blanks where another
woman's pictures marked the wall be the story
of how my edges caught fire and the ash at last
let me see where I stood. Let the cracked
kitchen floor make a map to teach me
where not to step, how not to fall through
and break my very own back.
Let the broken window be a way out,
the broken door a way in. Let me go
to the hardware store and buy the tools
to take the chain off the bedroom door,
let me paint the bathroom pink without asking,
walk naked and unafraid through all my rooms.

Let me pick up a broom and sweep
nothing under the rug. Let me sweep it all
into the light. Let me do it. Let there be time.
Let there be light.

On the Silence of Cotton

The big machines that rip
and comb and card,
the train cars and milling,
the dyeing vats—all that
noise and smell and heat
yet you come calm
and quiet into my house,
wound into skeins,
banded and mounded
into piles of reds and pinks,
violets and blues, cream
and browns and greens.

I offer the relief
of hands
after the big machines
and you, white-haired
wisdom of the field intact,
you offer my hands
back to me.

She Starts To Slow Down

For hurry is a form of violence and contrary
    to the laws of wholeness.

For the laws of wholeness are a pattern handed down,
    page after page of materials needed—
    yardage, colors and plies of thread, names of rivers,
    shapes of leaves, shapes of sentences and titles
    —the pages unnumbered and no instruction.

For there is no instruction on how to marry
    the work of the hands and the words
    of the river. By way of promise
    it can be done, only a needle with a bitten-off
    tail of thread stuck in the arm of an empty easy chair.

For the tale of thread goes back twenty thousand
    years—drop spindles spinning sixteen hours for the thread
    of single hour's weaving.

For a single hour's weaving is not to be entered
    into lightly but with all the gravity of the drop spindle,
    its tender weight, its small
      serious spin
        a world
          held
            holding
              held

Still Joy
for Amy

It was June again, towards the end,
all blue and green, full June, leaves shining
like droplets from a garden hose you waterfalled
through the morning sun into a backyard pool,
the kind you blow up ring by ring—remember now
the spatter sound of the first drops on plastic,
the beach ball smell of it, the endlessness
of summer?

It was my year to turn fifty and I wanted
to see things near as well as things far
so my younger daughter and I went walking
the three blocks to Walgreens, just down on the corner,
for reading glasses for me. I saw it
when we were five or six houses down—
a small, lady-sized chair, painted grass green
waiting at the edge of the sidewalk in a row
of mismatched end tables and empty baskets.
I want that, I said.

It was a rocker, I saw when we got closer.
What I love about a rocking chair
is how it lets you go
backward and forward, over and over
without ever leaving where you are. *I want that,*
I told my neighbor, and I gave my seven dollars
to her son who was watching over things and he set
the chair back from the sidewalk for us to pick up
on our way back.

It was a lucky morning, so I got blue
cats-eye glasses with sparkles in the corners.
And we got ice cream to walk back home with
because it was already about as hot as you could
stand, the sun that hot and bright. Drops of sweet
running from wrist to elbow and us trying
to eat fast and pick up the rocker at the same time—
she took one arm and I took the other and between us
we carried it through the morning
like a bride.

Harvest

All week long, the rain piles up dark
behind the mountains, showing itself
to us in fits and starts over the ridge
like an army waiting to invade, bolder
and bolder as reinforcements arrive
to bolster it from behind. We work
from dark to dark. Even in sleep
grain slips like water through my fingers,
pours out the corners of the pouch
I try to make from my skirt, the ache
of my back rolls into dream as thunder's
low groan.
         It is night
when we finish. Lentils and grain
bulge in their sacks, for once *enough*—
that word passes through the field
like a waterskin hand to hand, loosens
our breath, our shoulders, unknots
faces that for days on end have twisted
with work and worry, hurry and work.
We gather at the cookfire set up
in the low field. I sit on one side,
Rachel and Jacob on the other, leaning
into each other like those sacks of grain.
The rest of the household settles around,
children hiding at the edges,
jumping out to scare each other
in the dark.
         Except for Judah,
my Judah, six now and old enough
this year to help—so important,
so serious he was, carrying empty sacks
to us in the fields. His hard work

done now, he trails a stick in the dust
around and around the fire, singing
his own small song about fields
and beans and dirty knees. When he thinks
to look up, he sees me, his father,
Rachel, his grandmother, all eyes
on him—my beautiful,
beautiful boy—holding him there
at the center, by the fire that softens
even the hard pebbles of lentils
and makes them possible,
softens even the hard shell
of Rachel's eyes, that inner lid that closes
when my children come near, as though
to see them were to see a horror,
a shape of emptiness she could
never fill.
            But tonight, Judah circles
and he sees that we see him, we hold him
there in the warm, lit place, and his song begins
to grow, begins to spin out from the fire
like a swirl of sparks up into the dark, so unafraid
his joy in the moment I fear I will have to
look away.
           He stops,
shining, in front of me and I catch
my breath, he is about to speak, oh,
what can be the words for such
as this?

Mother,

    —he says, and I see
        only the knot of his two hands
           holding each other so tightly
              over his heart that his whole
                  small body tenses and shakes—

    I *am* *right* here.

Three Things That Happened Yesterday

I tried to do something really fast,
a sewing thing, like the Brave Little Tailor
only instead of giants—Twenty Coffee Cozies
At One Blow. I pinned them all in their rough-cut state
onto a long stretch of muslin on the quilting
machine and *Ready-Set-Go*. But their edges
curled around the hopping foot and stuck
the needle every time till finally near the end
the needle broke and ruined one little brown
calico cozy with round orange and yellow-gold
flowers on spiky light green stems.
You better stop. I said it out loud several times
until I listened and went upstairs to find lunch.

I had egg salad and tomato soup from a can
which, I have a friend who says *Life's too short
to eat bad food*, but I have another friend
who says, *Oh, I love that stuff, I don't
care.* Neither one was the friend
who called right after lunch to tell me
she'd heard the post office lady explain
to some Mexicans trying to send a giant
box back home, *You have to understand,
there's no surface anymore, there's only air.*
I sat on the floor under the wall phone
in the kitchen and we thought about that
till she had to go wash her hair and sure enough,
later that night, she sent me a poem through the air—
it landed on my screen, blew out
of her hairdryer, is what she said.

When I hung up the phone after lunch I didn't know
what to do with myself, I couldn't get a hold

on anything, but I needed black yarn and
it's hardly ever wrong, I told myself, to go buy yarn.
So I went to the little Jo-Ann's nearby, where I
used to work, hoping they'd have it and I'd not
have to drive all the way up to the big store in Hudson
and *Hurray!* they had it and I had many coupons and also
it was all on sale so I got the black I needed plus a big
bunch of variegateds in blues and plummy purples,
coppers and greens, and five or six more
that looked like harvest or straw-into-gold.
I heaped my basket high and when I went
to check out, Sherry and Liz said,
How're those grandbabies doing? I told them
all about how big the boys are, and what the boys are saying now,
and they smiled at me, those two women,
the way you smile at happiness you understand.
Then I said bye and walked out the double doors
with my big bag of yarn, all those colors, and
You just won't believe, I told the yarn as
I set the bag in the car beside me,
all the things you are going to be.

Lots of Ships

Lots of ships have already sailed and I wasn't on any of them and none came to save me from anything I've wanted rescued from. Once I thought of a front porch as a ship, the rising and falling torrent of leaves on the hill beyond the porch rail as waves breaking at the prow. I was reaching, I think, the page so new to me then and all my pens and pencils rowing for some kind of shore. That was a mistake, you know, almost always it's out to sea you want to be rowing. Almost always I can't abide greeting cards but a few weeks ago I came across this at the drugstore—two amphibious looking creatures like you've never seen before standing on a rock with flood waters rising all around and the ark afloat out in the distance. *Oh, crap*, one says to the other. *Was that today?* It made me laugh so I brought it home and stuck it on the fridge with a little calendar magnet from the insurance company—but that's how easy it is to die, that little forgetting. All ships are she, a poet I once met said. She came walking up behind me one summer on a college sidewalk with a friend and as she caught up she said, *How old will you be forever?* I said *Fifteen*, and she said to her friend, *See, I told you she'd know what I meant*. That was a good ship, alright. I am still trying to name her.

It's Not Up To You, Sweetheart

Do you ever wake up in the morning
and read a poem first thing
then all day long your thoughts
are trying to shape themselves
into lines? And if it's Dickinson,
do you notice your grocery list starts
to fall into hymn meter, and one
missed syllable leaves you all day feeling
like you forgot something?
Those days, even when you have a lot
to do, do you find you are pausing
at places you'd never thought
to pause before? Or find yourself
in line at the bank with a voice
in your head, the poet who somehow says
the silence along with the words,
filling you with a quiet that makes it
impossible to be afraid of anything?
And then do your thoughts really
begin to break and break?

Small Song, or, Cosmology

Oh, sweet
slip of soul
married to me
for your turn
in this world,
I offer you
my heart
like a womb.
I offer breath
and throat
for whatever
song you want
to sing, fingers
to spell out
whatever words
you know.
I offer
crooked feet
on a crooked
road and when
I go, when I go,
    will you have me?
        Will you hold?

How I Don't Know

This is the way I don't know anything:
I add the same column of numbers
over and over, I listen to songs
about the old sea, startle to find
myself rooting around in the cupboards.
What are you looking for? I ask,
and I don't know. *Well, what
might not be wrong?* I ask. Maybe
knitting, maybe walking to the library.

This is the way I walk to the library:
in a circle there and back, taking
steps. Threading the bead
of walking to the library onto
the circlet of my day. The more
beads you thread onto a bracelet,
the bigger it gets, too many
and it slides right off, the way
my days get by me and by me
and still I don't know
how to figure out what it is
I need.

This is how I talk to God about it all:
a little too fast, a little too wild—
daily bread—daily—okay—okay

Some Things the Doorways Want To Tell Us

We don't appear
to eyes
except in dreams.

Have you never dreamed
a tiny opening, high up
near a ceiling,
on the other side
something
utterly else?

We appear, as you say,
like the teacher
when the student is ready.

Do not confuse us
with doors.

It is the hardest thing,
this holding open
of everything
with nothing.

Maybe This Will Help

Last week I saw a boy walking home from school
by the side of a busy road, walking against traffic
like he must have been told. On his side of the road,
red flamey leaves hung onto maple trees, the sky
was bright October blue-for-boy. He looked
to be about thirteen, was looking all around,
bare-faced and grinny. His coat was thrown open,
his head thrown back and tossing from side to side,
from time to time his arms lifted and flourished
like a magic wand or a conductor's wand and he was singing,
right out loud like no one was watching, singing
right out loud for all he was worth.

Or this—
Once I dreamed a beautiful white-haired
woman, speaking to a crowd under a tree.
She had a formula, she had a way
of writing books, books everyone would want
to read, to buy, so if you could learn to write
her way, soon enough you'd have
all the money you'd need. But I came late
to the meeting. By the time I reached
the edge of the crowd already she was
being hurried away. I ran after her, shouting,
so great was my need. She wouldn't
stop for me, but she turned her head
and called back over her shoulder,
Just write me twenty or thirty
beautiful words.

As for the laying on of hands,
I know of a place here in the center
of town where if you stand

in the clear, palms up
and full of black oil sunflower seeds,
chickadees will come and light
and eat from your hand.
Next time you come,
I'll take you there.

Where I'm From
after George Ella Lyon

I am from Hopie and Odell, from Rumi's anteroom
    of souls—some kind of late night wedding chapel
    where, as my parents married, my soul stood up
    at the sweetness of their faces. *Yes,* I said.
    I will. I do.

I am from Sweet Jesus glowing honey brown
    on the back wall of the church, and my mother's cousin
    Darlene leading song service up front, her arms
    waving like a drum major's—
    I'm redeemed   by love divine
        I'm redeemed   by love divine
    Glory, Glory, Christ is mine, Christ is mine
    —the men singing the echo part and the sun
    pouring in all wild.

I am from the uncool table of girls who polished rocks,
    made up songs in little notebooks and spoke in the language
    of *The Once and Future King*. From learning to say *Grandma*
    instead of *Mamaw,* and to not tell about the poke
    Daddy pulled from the side of the road for supper. I am from
    the time I asked Laura Grinstead of the smooth hair
    and matching clothes a question about English class,
    and Nancy Grimm informed me: *Were you talking to her?*
    I am from watching my sister-in-law to learn what to wear.

I am from ten years of graduate school and always only one
    right answer for every twenty-five students, from the full professor
    who said to me, as I sat in his office eight months gone—shame
    I was having babies instead of books.

I am from my girls who birth me every day into this world.

I am from heart attacks and strokes, from Daddy playing his guitar
    and whispering hope to Uncle Ted at three a.m.
    in the Morrow County hospital, and from my cousin Debby
    who punched out the nurse that tried to stop him.
    I am from the man who took off his hat when I cried
    in the elevator in Saint Joe's and from the woman
    who prayed with my mother in the bathroom at Walmart
    the fourth day after chemo.

I am from the same waiting room
    as you—the one where God said *Who will go*
    to this world I made only out of things that die
    and find out for us how much sweetness that adds?
    And we all of us raised our hands.

An Invisible Story

I learned this week from my reading
on the shadow that each person has an invisible
tree growing inside, making the kind
of progress that needs to be made no matter
what is happening on the outside.
And if a person goes long enough
without looking to that tree, well,
that's when you get
nailed to it.
                This makes me want to learn
all the shapes of all the leaves
and the names of trees and to take
a pen-and-ink drawing class so my hand
might know as well as my head about all the choices
a tree can make.
                    It makes me want to drive
over to the grade school in early October
and walk the sidewalks home with first-grade eyes,
on the lookout always for sugar maples, fiery orange leaves
still tinged with green, the trees' hands outstretched,
splayed, burning to tell me what all I don't know
about my story on the inside.

Or Else

It is not a tree at all, but an old,
old woman at a spinning wheel
working without words,
without hurry and without cease
in the shadow back behind your heart.

Some days you almost hear
the hum of the wheel, your thoughts
twist, in your steps you feel
the treadle pulse.

Ask her whatever you want, the answer
is always the same—work
in the shadow back behind your heart
without words, without hurry or cease.

The Apple

A woman who says she is
your sister knocks on your door
with a basket of apples
on her arm. She remembers you,
she says, from before,
from another time when things
were very different, both of you
so young when all of it happened, all of it
so long ago. She's ready now, she says.
The circle could be unbroken
if only you
would do
what Jesus would do.

And I brought you these,
she says, feeling around
in the basket of apples for the roundest
reddest shiniest one. *Go ahead*,
she says. *Take it. Take a bite.
Just one bite and swallow
and it can all
be put right.*

Sorting the Seeds

That is exactly the work of sorting the seeds, trying to become conscious down to the very bottom of the situation and then to know what's what, and what has what effect ... to do it for a long time would be the woman's heroic deed.
    —Marie-Louise Von Franz

Just like nothing ever happened,
    my father says. I told her that's the only way
    for her to come back.

My mother dreams the cat is dead
    but still, when she goes out to save the kittens,
    it fastens all its claws into her leg,
    still it terrorizes her and she wakes up screaming
    Get it off—Get it off—

How my sister's mouth pinched that terrible year
    when my mother, who knew already
    what my sister was doing, offered to help me
    clean my house.

The husband doesn't knock
    on front doors, he stands on tiptoe
    to look through a window and taps
    on the pane. Inside the house
    he talks through doors, and against
    anything locked, he rages.

For seven days I clean
    the basement—scraps of leather,
    knives, archeological trash, toys,
    outgrown clothes, folders and folders
    of old school files, piles of bedding,
    dirty laundry, a mountain of black
    trash bags out the back door.

Something like that happened
    in my marriage, says a woman
    at the end of that summer. *And was it*
    your sister? I ask. *No,* she says.
    It was my best friend,
    I don't have a sister.

The garbage bags unmoved from the back door
    when I get home from the mountains.
    The basement flooded,
    floating with ruin.

Way Down at the Bottom of Everything Where It's All Mixed Up and Everyone Is Everyone

I meet my sister. As long as we're here,
I tell her, I might as well say it out loud—
I never liked you. You had a way
of looking on me in my distress.
You threatened calamity
when it seemed you might not
get your way. *You don't understand
what you're doing*, is what you'd say.
Oh, I remember it all, how you went
from room to room telling each one
the other said this, the other said that.
You knifed the couch, you knifed the chairs.
Be careful, you said.
      Way down here
at the bottom of everything, everyone
has a knife, everyone has a way.
You keep talking, you keep saying
whatever it was you said. You
keep on, you don't understand—
down here, at bottom, you're dead.

Begotten

I am the daughter of Laban, and of my mother whose name is lost,
    and of this name, Leah, by which my father increased his fold
    but I have another name, from the story before the story they made.

I am the daughter of Cain for my spirit wanders, but my garment
    unravels a thin thread of grief leading me always back to their fires.

I am the daughter of the sins of my father but my blood is a rope
    I cannot cut and I shudder at its spillage from the coil
    of my heart, from the knot of my womb.

I am the daughter of my mother's loom, the memory of color in the folds
    of her clothes; daughter of all my mothers' looms, though my own hands
    know better. I stream from all the mothers before me and I pray
    my small fork lead the river astray.

I am the daughter of flood, of river rock in the field, dry boat
    on the mountaintop; daughter of the raven, returned.

I am daughter of salt hardened into the shape of a wife, for such
    is the cost of looking; daughter of thresholds but always
    I wake at the moment of crossing.

I am begotten of the daughters of Lot, for no stranger appears at my well,
    yet my children must be brought.

I am the daughter of fields terraced like ziggurats up the side
    of the mountain, offerings to the feet of their god, but I stand
    with my arms wrapped around my heart.

I am daughter of the law, yet I am hated; daughter of many eyes,
    yet my own are hooded. I am the daughter of grief but I have
    sewn shut my mouth.

I am the daughter of She Who Hears Me, but though I open
    and open I will not be fed. Daughter of the Father,
    but though I close and clench I will not be spared.

I am the daughter of knives and Rachel and Rachel's beauty,
    and I cannot cut my way through the thick
    caul of my sister's story, both of us

Begotten of Hagar and Sarai, who heed not the crying out
    of blood from the ground again and again, who tremble not
    at the wrestlings of angels or of brothers, who scoff
    at the wars of men.

Stones

After nearly thirty years, the sister reappeared dragging behind her a large cloth sack. The sack was so heavy and full of stones that you could see exactly where she was coming from, everything in the path behind her lay flattened and dead. At first she stood in the road before the woman's house and asked to be let in. By this time the woman had lived seven years in her house alone and she knew that what she didn't want need not be invited in. When she didn't answer, the sister came closer, up near the climbing rose that grew over the side of the porch by the front window. *I have something for you*, she said, pointing to the sack of stones, for each stone was a story she told about how she hadn't really done anything she had done. *Those aren't my stones*, said the woman to herself and still she didn't answer. The sister became very angry because more than anything she wanted someone else to carry those stones, she didn't like people to be able to see exactly where it was she was coming from. She pulled a large stone out of the bag and hurled it at the window, but it bounced back to her because the window was perfectly clear about who had done what. She threw more stones, thinking that surely one would break through but none, large or small, could get inside. Finally there was nothing for her to do but pick them up and go back the way she came, still dragging the large cloth sack and adding to it new stones for this part of the story. Inside, the woman walked slowly through her rooms, looking at everything each one held, moving small things around here and there and deciding what to do with the rest of her days.

IV
After

Psalm of Leah

> *Leah . . . . Rachel. The names mean "cow" and "ewe" respectively.*
> —*Zondervan NIV Study Bible*

You Who Hear Me,
though my name is only the sound
of the low groan in the field, the rip
of grass from the ground, the obscene
wail of the one
cut off from the herd; You
Who See the wince
of the small humiliation of milking,
the twisted grimace of husbandry,
the face beaten like a plowshare
into the shape of what happens to it;

I know

You are not the stone eyes of my father's
small gods, You are nothing
Rachel can steal. You are not the stones Jacob
heaps as altars over top his sins
to mark his trail. You are not the stone
from the mountain broken, You are the mountain
broken, its face undone, the space left open
when the men with the hammers have gone.

I and Thou

When one says You, the I of the word pair I-you is said, too ...
The basic word I-You can only be spoken with one's whole being.
—Martin Buber

When I tell you it's a beautiful morning
here, what I mean is September
and blackbirds sounding the distances
between everything, and everything is
getting a little farther away but I can
love the blackbirds too. It's their turn,
they should have it. I am writing to you
with the green pen you gave me, so
you know whatever the words,
they're all calling on mercy, mercy
being one of those graces that doesn't care
who calls and who answers—the honeysuckle
has taken over the glider, is what I write.
And if I send you a picture of us sitting
together at a big round table looking at
poems under a double wedding ring quilt hung
on the wall, or of us staring wide-eyed
at each other in a hotel elevator
with a beautiful young pregnant woman,
or in a little hilly graveyard tucked just
back beyond the hardware store, somewhere
in those pictures there is another one—
a first grade, postage stamp–sized
black and white of either of us
with crooked, too-short bangs
and doubtful eyes. She loves you,
is what I'm saying. Tuck her picture
into your mirror, is what I mean.

Soul Retrieval

Imagine a woman walking through her house,
nighttime, summer. If there are children
they are sleeping in the small boats of the their beds,
she alone is moving through this liquid time for which
there is no word, when deepest blue arrives
as black. If there is anything in the house
that makes noise, it is shut off, only the sounds
that sift up from the grass wash through the curtains
like small, laced-edged waves, the windows left open
till the last. She circles wordlessly through her rooms
picking up each loose thing she finds on the floor,
the couch, kitchen table, bottom stair and piles it
into the bottomless basket she has made from the crook
of her left arm. In her wake, lamps switched off,
she leaves the dark. The closest she comes to you,
who watch her window from the street, is when,
one arm loaded with all she has picked up, she turns
sideways to the window and with her free arm
pulls down the pane, twists the small lock
and draws the curtain closed. Only
in the moment of her twisting the lock
do you understand she is you, your whole soul
gathered into the sweet moist crook of her arm,
all your parts, everything you need, in that house
you thought was only imagined.

Leaving the Story

You will never not know
that the castle is there, the keep still keeping
certain ghosts who fear dark roads
more than dark walls, whose loneliness
thunders through the halls.

Below, the kitchen is cold. You see
the corners of the rugs have all been lifted
and the floors unswept by some kind
and helpful spirit so that simply by coming
down the steps from the keep you find
the breadcrumbs
meant to lead you out
of this enchantment, your own,
whatever it is.
                The door opens
when you touch it. It is not wrong
to pause on the threshold, here at the very
end of the story. Behind you, everything *ever*.
Before you, on the dark road,
everything *after*.

Notes

"Lots of Ships." This poem references *Why The Ships Are She* by Terri Ford.

"An Invisible Story." The image of the tree comes from Jung, through Marie-Louise von Franz, who says in *Shadow and Evil in Fairy Tales,* "Jung shows that the tree symbolizes human life and development and the inner process of becoming conscious. One could say that it symbolizes in the psyche that something which grows and develops undisturbed within us, irrespective of what the ego does; it is the urge toward individuation which unfolds and continues, independent of our consciousness."

"Way Down at the Bottom of Everything, Where It's All Mixed Up and Everyone Is Everyone." The words of this title are borrowed from Kumkum Malik. The language "looking on me in my distress" is borrowed from the fairy tale "The Black Woman's Castle."

Acknowledgments

I'm grateful to the editors of the following journals in which some of these poems first appeared: *Appalachian Journal*: "Tender"; *Cerise Press*: "Where I'm From"; *Cortland Review*: "Harvest"; *Crab Orchard Review*: "The Naming of the Scars"; *Massachusetts Review*: "Psalm of Leah"; and from *Ploughshares*: "Leah Will Say Nothing" and "Ringstraked." "The Father's Story" first appeared under a different title in my first book, *One of Everything*.

I wrote this book with the help of A Room of Her Own Foundation. The AROHO Gift of Freedom supported me financially for two years while I wrote and AROHO continues to support me professionally and spiritually. The leadership, Darlene Chandler Bassett, Mary Johnson, Kate Gale and Tracey Cravens-Gras, and the AROHO community have been a source of friendship and wisdom I could not do without. My life on and off the page is sweeter and richer for their presence in it.

Biographical Note

Diane Gilliam is the author of three previous collections of poetry: *Kettle Bottom*, *One of Everything*, and *Recipe for Blackberry Cake* (chapbook). She holds an MFA from Warren Wilson College and a PhD in Romance Languages and Literatures from Ohio State University. She has received an Individual Artist Grant from the Ohio Arts Council, the Chaffin Award for Appalachian Writing, and a Pushcart Prize. She is the most recent recipient of the $50,000 Gift of Freedom literary prize from the A Room of Her Own Foundation.

www.ingramcontent.com/pod-product-compliance
Ingram Content Group UK Ltd.
Pitfield, Milton Keynes, MK11 3LW, UK
UKHW041938210426
5322IPUK00016B/247